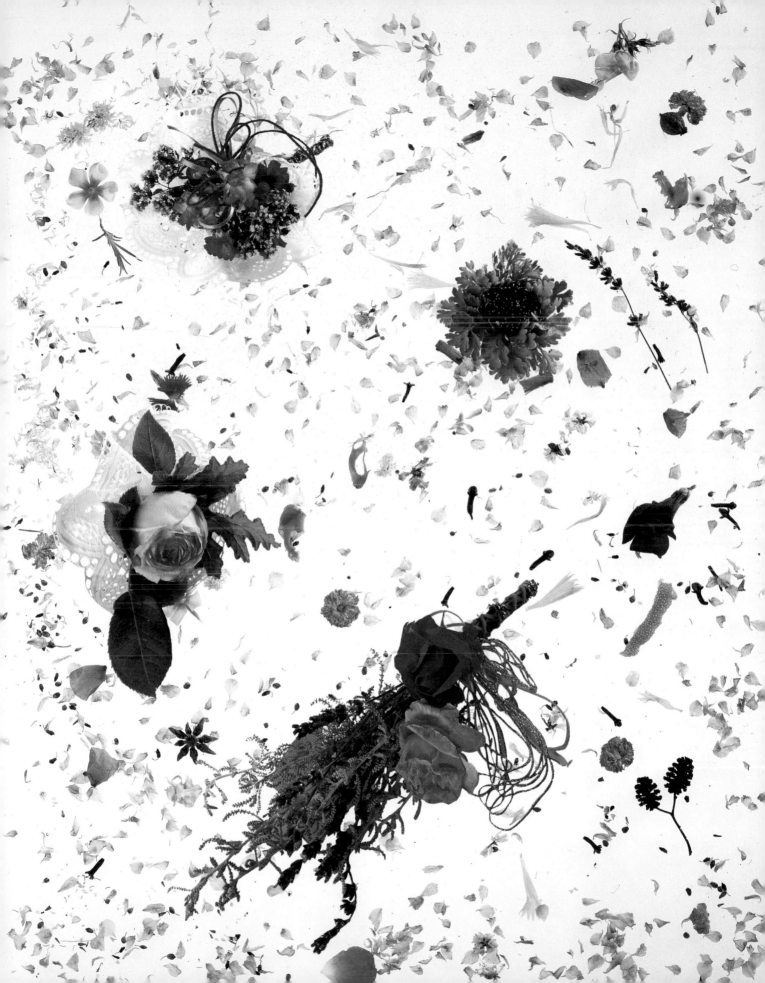

Anne Effelsberg

HOW TO DESIGN & MAKE

POTPOURRI
& SCENTED BOUQUETS

AN ILLUSTRATED GUIDE

CRESCENT BOOKS
NEW YORK • AVENEL, NEW JERSEY

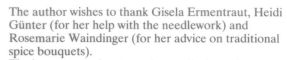

The author wishes to thank Gisela Ermentraut, Heidi Günter (for her help with the needlework) and Rosemarie Waindinger (for her advice on traditional spice bouquets).

The bouquets and potpourri were displayed in a range of dishes, vases and containers, supplied by – among others – "Casa Bea", Klosterhofweg 74, 4050 Mönchengladbach (pages 45, 52, 67, 69, 74); Handelskontor Haymann, Auf der Heide, 5239 Norken (pages 36, 37, 43); Andrea Schweizer, Rosental 101, 5300 Bonn (pages 50, 51), and "Allerlei", Laakstrasse 42, 4223 Voerde (pages 32, 48, 59, 60, 64).

Preserving agents, fixatives and essential oils were supplied by Josefa Dürolf, Rabegasse 19, 6310 Grünberg, Hessen.

Grateful thanks to all of the above companies for their most generous support.

(Preserving agents, fixatives and essential oils can all be obtained from local druggists and floral supply stores. The essential oils can also be obtained from natural perfume, cosmetic or health-food stores.)

Published in Germany in 1992 by Falken–Verlag GmbH, 6272 Niedernhausen/Ts.

Published in the UK in 1993 by Transedition Books, 11–15 The Vineyard, Abingdon, Oxon OX14 3XB.

German language edition and photographs © Falken–Verlag GmbH 1993

American language edition © Transedition Books 1993

Title photograph by: TLC Foto-Studio GmbH, Velen-Ramsdorf. All other photographs by TLC Foto-Studio GmbH, Velen-Ramsdorf, with the exception of that on the right hand side of page 19, Falken Archiv/Arius. Drawings by Daniela Schneider, Frankfurt/Main. *Layout:* Ilse Stockmann-Sauer, AS–Design, Offenbach.

This 1993 edition published in the USA by Crescent Books, distributed by Outlet Book Company, Inc., a Random House Company, 40 Engelhard Avenue, Avenel, New Jersey 07001, Random House
New York • Toronto • London • Sydney • Auckland

ISBN 0–517–08790–1

Printed in 1993 in Slovenia

CONTENTS

TEMPTING FRAGRANCES

Inspirational ideas and illustrations to

create beautiful, scented decorations for

the home from dried and fresh flowers,

spices, and plant material.

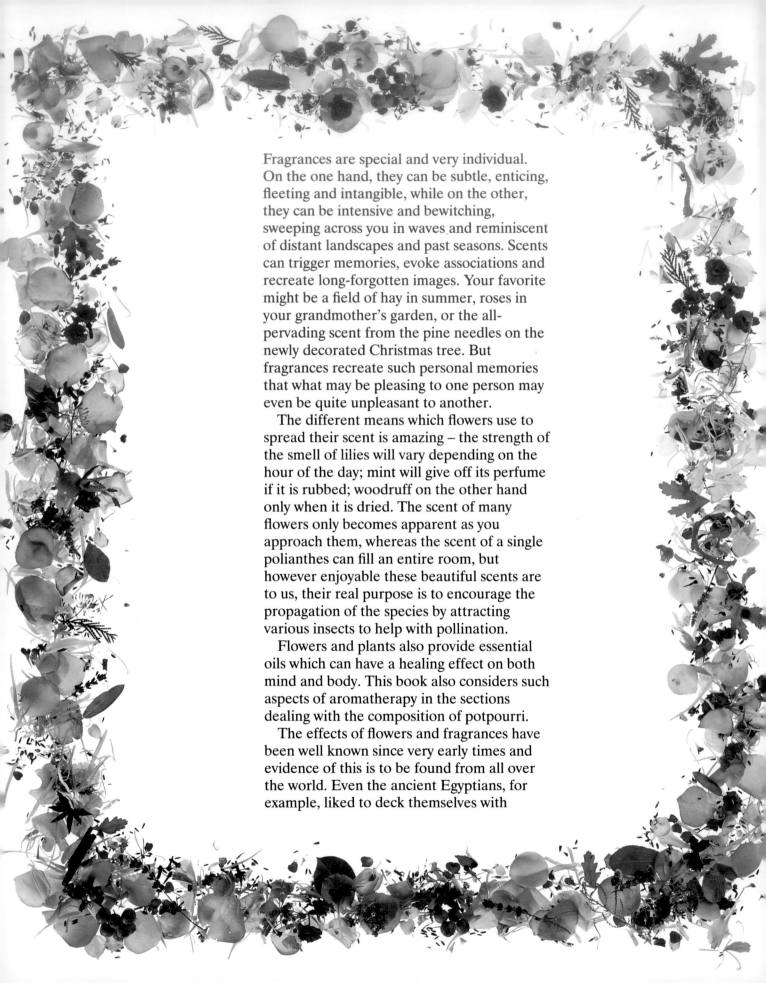

Fragrances are special and very individual. On the one hand, they can be subtle, enticing, fleeting and intangible, while on the other, they can be intensive and bewitching, sweeping across you in waves and reminiscent of distant landscapes and past seasons. Scents can trigger memories, evoke associations and recreate long-forgotten images. Your favorite might be a field of hay in summer, roses in your grandmother's garden, or the all-pervading scent from the pine needles on the newly decorated Christmas tree. But fragrances recreate such personal memories that what may be pleasing to one person may even be quite unpleasant to another.

The different means which flowers use to spread their scent is amazing – the strength of the smell of lilies will vary depending on the hour of the day; mint will give off its perfume if it is rubbed; woodruff on the other hand only when it is dried. The scent of many flowers only becomes apparent as you approach them, whereas the scent of a single polianthes can fill an entire room, but however enjoyable these beautiful scents are to us, their real purpose is to encourage the propagation of the species by attracting various insects to help with pollination.

Flowers and plants also provide essential oils which can have a healing effect on both mind and body. This book also considers such aspects of aromatherapy in the sections dealing with the composition of potpourri.

The effects of flowers and fragrances have been well known since very early times and evidence of this is to be found from all over the world. Even the ancient Egyptians, for example, liked to deck themselves with

exotically perfumed lotus garlands, while the Romans were renowned for their sumptuous rose festivals. Perfumed incense was also regularly burned in honor of the gods.

In Europe, the interest in fragrances began during the Middle Ages, which is not surprising given the standards of hygiene of the times. People used to wear sweetly scented items, such as necklaces and gloves, and carry aptly named nosegays. They would powder their hair and even sprinkled perfume into the public water supply during festivals.

Many of the terms that we use today have origins that can be traced back to these early days. For example, the word "potpourri" comes from the French "pot" (pot) and "pourri" (rotten) and literally means "rotten pot". This description is understandable, if we remember that it used to refer to the "fermented" potpourri, that was always damp and had a very unattractive, brown and moldy appearance. Nowadays, we understand the word "pomander" as signifying a preserved citrus fruit that has been studded with cloves, but the name comes from the Middle Ages when people used to wear sweet smelling garlands made of apple-shaped objects in order to ward off disease. These were filled with perfumes such as amber. The French term "pomme d'ambre" ("apple of amber"), has now become "pomander". Many examples of these perfumed garlands can be seen in medieval paintings.

Once you have begun to discover the delightful world of floral fragrances you will find more and more to interest you. I hope that this book will inspire you to make discoveries of your own.

Flowers, herbs and spices –
characteristics of their fragrance
and their symbolic meanings:

Camellia	Friendly, warm, spicy and fruity I am concerned for you
Carnation	Slightly dry, flowery with a hint of pepper. In constant longing
Cinnamon	Full, intense, warm and spicy. Warmth and calm
Clove	Dry, spicy and warm. Make way for the new and cast out the old
Elderflower	A full, heady and flowery perfume The first awakening of love
Eucalyptus	Like camphor, stimulating and fresh I wish you well
Guelder rose	Sweet yet a little bitter Gentle but fun
Hay	A full, dry, cheerful scent of summer Silent and tender togetherness
Honeysuckle	Full, sensuous and heady Bewitching
Lavender	Spicy and fresh Chasing away gloom
Lemon-scented pelargonium	Intense, fresh and lemony Spoil yourself
Lily, White	A full, sweet and heavy perfume Pure love
Lily of the Valley	Charming, light, intense and flowery Happiness will return
Meadowsweet	Friendly and prickly-sweet Tender thoughts of you
Mint	Lemony and refreshing Wisdom in life
Myrtle	Slightly herb-like yet appealing Eternally bound together
Nutmeg	Aromatic, spicy and tangy Restrain yourself

Peony	Full, fresh, powerful and flowery A full and powerful life
Peppermint	Refreshing, spicy and friendly Knowledge
Polianthes	Intense, full, bewitching scent Uninhibited, unbridled pleasure
Rose, Red	Intense, appealing and flowery Unlimited love
Rosemary	Pungent and aromatic Remembrance
Sweet pea	Attractively soft and cheerful, with a hint of cinnamon. Gentle cheerfulness
Star anise	Full spicy aroma with a hint of amber Near yet far
Stephanotis	Powerful, enveloping scent Crowning glory
Stock	Penetrating, flowery with a hint of clove. Powerful beauty
Tansy (Common) or Golden Buttons	Healthy-like camphor, spicy Be brave
Thyme	Intense, herb-like and friendly Beside you
Vetch	Fresh, light and flowery A farewell and a new start
Violet	Slightly sweet, gentle and tender Blooming in secret
Virgin's Bower	Attractive with a sharp undercurrent Living together in peace
Wallflower	Warm fragrance Lovingly one with you
Walnut	Independent, warm and tangy In spite of everything
Wormwood	Slightly acrid, fresh and spicy Trust
Yarrow	Spicy, like camphor, but not penetrating. I often think of you
Yellow Bedstraw	Soft, bright and gentle-like woodruff We shall find a way

GENERAL INFORMATION

A guide to flowers, herbs and spices, the

techniques of preserving and wiring and

also tying and arranging posies and

bouquets.

FLOWERS

The first thing you should do with fresh flowers is remove all the leaves from the lower stalk and some from the upper stalk. Each stem should not be snapped off but cut obliquely with a sharp knife. If the stems are woody – shrubs, chrysanthemums and roses, for instance – slit them for about 1 inch. Put the flowers directly into water. It is even better, if the stems can be cut under running water. Ideally, put flowers into water that has stood for 12 hours after being boiled. They do not like ice cold water. Before starting your arrangement, the flowers should be stood in deep water for 1–2 hours in a cool place. Take time with your preparations and your flowers will last longer.

Don't leave flowers out of water unnecessarily. For example, when you are tying a bunch, leave the flowers to stand in a bucket of water until you need them.

Flowers give off their fragrance at different times of the year. Violets, vetch, hyacinths, lilac, freesias, lilies of the valley, guelder roses, wallflowers and narcissus are all early spring flowers, whereas peonies, camellias, jasmine, reseda (mignonette), sweet peas and honeysuckle bloom in the early summer. Marigolds, roses, carnations, lavender and the others in the photograph flower in high summer.

Not to be forgotten are the highly scented "green" plant materials, such as the needles from pine, cedar or larch trees. The leaves of the fragrant pelargonium, eucalyptus, and artemisia will enhance any arrangement with their characteristic perfumes. There are many aromatic herbs and spices, such as coriander, nutmeg, cloves, thyme, laurel and citrus fruits, which are used in several of the potpourri and bouquets described in this book.

If you cannot find a particular flower recommended for an arrangement, or if it is out of season then use whatever you have or your own special favorites.

11. Carnation (Dianthus caryophyllus)
12. Virgin's Bower (Clematis vitalba)
13. Lavender (Lavandula angustifolia)
14. Feverfew (Chrysanthemum parthenium)
15. Sweet Orange (Citrus sinensis)
16. Heliotrope or Cherry Pie (Heliotropium arborescens)
17. Sweet Scabious (Scabiosa atropurpurea)
18. Yellow Bedstraw (Galium verum)
19. Candytuft (Iberis arendsii)
20. Bourbon Rose (Rosa borboniana "La Reine Victoria")
21. Honeysuckle (Lonicera tellmanniana)
22. Summer Phlox (Phlox paniculata)
23. Madonna lily (Lilium candidum)
24. Common Oleander or Rosebay (Nerium oleander)
25. Nasturtium (Tropaeolum majus)
26. Charles Austin rose (Rosa-Gardenrose "Charles Austin")
27. Centaurea (Centaurea montana)
28. Privet (Ligustrum vulgare)
29. Common Tansy or Golden Buttons (Tanacetum vulgare)
30. Regal or Royal lily (Lilium regale)
31. Butterfly bush (Buddleia davidii)
32. Pot marigold (Calendula officinalis)

1. Spotted deadnettle (Lamium maculatum)
2. Fern-leaf Yarrow (Achillea filipendulina)
3. Corn marigold (Chrysanthemum segetum)
4. Oswego Tea plant (Monarda didyma)
5. Cape leadwort (Plumbago auriculata)

6. Flossflower (Ageratum houstonianum)
7. Wintergreen or Checkerberry (Gaultheria procumbens)
8. Meadowsweet (Filipendula ulmaria)
9. Wax plant (Hoya carnosa)
10. Yellow Sage (Lantana-Camara hybrids)

SPICES

1. Orange (Citrus sinensis)
2. Kumquat (Fortunella japonica)
3. Grapefruit (Citrus maxima)
4. Mandarin (Citrus reticulata)
5. Lime (Citrus aurantiifolia)
6. Lemon (Citrus limon)
7. Cinnamon (Cinnamomum verum)
8. Nutmeg (Myristica fragrans)
9. Coriander (Coriander sativum)
10. Mace/nutmeg flower (Myristicum fragrans)
11. Juniper (Juniperis communis)
12. Paprika (Capsicum annuum)
13. Star anise (Illicum verum)
14. Allspice (Pimenta dioica)
15. Clove (Syzygium aromaticum)
16. Vanilla (Vanilla planifolia)
17. Cardamom (Elettaria cardamomum)
18. Bay leaves (Laurus nobilis)
19. Chili (Capsicum frutescens)

1. Mugwort (Artemisia vulgaris)
2. Lovage (Levisticum officinalis)
3. Germander (Teucrium chamaedrys)
4. Cypress grass (Santolina chamaecyparissus)
5. Hyssop (Hyssopus officinalis)
6. Thyme (Thymus vulgaris)
7. Lemon balm (Melissa officinalis)
8. Borage (Borago officinalis)
9. Lemon verbena (Verbena hybrids)
10. Woodruff (Galium odoratum)
11. Tarragon (Artemisia dracunculus)
12. Rue (Ruta graveolens)
13. Chives (Allium schoenoprasum)
14. Marjoram (Origanum majorana)
15. Pimpernel (Pimpinella major)
16. Bay (Laurus nobilis)
17. Rosemary (Rosmarinus officinalis)
18. Apple Mint (Mentha suaveolens)
19. European mint (Mentha longifolia)
20. Common sage (Salvia officinalis)
21. Clary (Salvia sclarea)

HERBS

PRESERVING FLOWERS

The ability to keep a beautiful flower, a fine specimen of a peony or rose for example, beyond its normal life-span is exactly what makes preserving flowers so attractive. Of course, the colors, size and also surface texture of a flower will all change in the process. The flower develops a muted and more fragile appearance. Possibly within a matter of months, but in any case within a couple of years, it will have turned a dull pale brown and this is the time to make a new arrangement or potpourri.

I get a great deal of pleasure at this stage: deciding on my method of preservation and the individual jobs to be done, the excitement of waiting to see how the dried flowers look and last of all the arranging itself. It is exactly all this preparatory work with the flowers themselves that can make drying flowers such an extremely relaxing and pleasant occupation. Below, are some of my favorite methods of preserving and drying flowers.

Flowers left to dry on a window sill or sideboard or hung up in bunches from the ceiling still look pretty and make a colorful room decoration.

DRYING FLAT

With this method you will be able to dry petals, leaves and flower heads very effectively. Simply spread out the plant material in a warm, dry place. You need a well ventilated working area so do not use closed containers. Flat, perforated cardboard boxes are ideal for this purpose or you can use sheets of newspaper. However, you will get a more professional effect if you use a fine wire mesh stretched across a wooden frame.

Drying usually takes between two days and a week, depending upon the type of plant material and conditions of drying, but when ready the material should feel crisp. Flower heads should be arranged facing upward; leaves and petals should be thinly spread out and stirred gently each day. On a fine summer's day, I dry large quantities of flowers quickly by spreading them out on a blanket in the sun.

You can display and dry flowers even more quickly if you pop them in your oven or even a micro-wave oven. Flowers dry quickly and easily at lower temperatures (120°F), and especially if you have an air circulating oven. Do keep a watchful eye on them all the time! Drying time can be between 30 minutes and several hours. (I suggest you experiment first with several types of blooms at various temperatures and for different lengths of time, as all ovens are different.)

LEAVING THE FLOWERS TO STAND

Once the flowers have faded completely, the water level in the container will fall dramatically depending on the size of the bunch. This allows the flowers to dry out gradually but keep out of direct sunlight to preserve the color.

The preservation process can be assisted by placing the flowers against a warm background (for example, a radiator). If a wet foam block is used, no further water should be added once the flowers have completely faded.

HANGING

A warm, dry and well ventilated room, an attic for example, is the ideal place to hang bunches of flowers and herbs. Try to keep them out of direct sunlight or they will start to bleach. In summer time, I use the principle of the "baker's oven" and hang my flowers out to dry on a clothes drier. Nothing could be simpler! Firstly, remove most of the leaves from the stem and secure the bunches with a rubber band – to prevent rotting keep the bunches small and the flower heads at varying levels to encourage air circulation and even drying – then suspend them upside down on a piece of strong wire that has been bent into the shape of a hook.

SILICA GEL CRYSTALS

Visually, you can get very attractive results by using silica gel crystals (blue gel) for drying flowers. These are available in the form of pale blue or white crystals and they absorb all surrounding moisture. Scatter a shallow layer of crystals across the base of a container and then place the flowers one by one into the container. Carefully cover with a further layer of crystals making sure that the crystals get within the petals. Then close the container tightly. Within a few days the flowers will have dried completely. You can check this by looking at the color of the crystals, which will turn pink as the flowers gradually lose their moisture. Remove the silica gel crystals with a spoon (or a cup), or alternatively gently shake them out. But take care, because these crystals give off an unpleasant dust. You will marvel at the quality of the dried flowers, especially those kinds, such as orchids, lilies or gerberas, which are normally very difficult to dry. Depending on the size of the flowers, you will need about 1 lb of silica gel from the druggist to dry each batch.

The moisture can subsequently be extracted from the crystals by spreading them on a dry baking sheet and warming in the oven. Afterward they should be stored in sealed containers. Although the initial cost is high, the crystals can be used over and over again.

IMMERSION TECHNIQUES

Another age-old method of preserving flowers is to immerse them in liquid wax. This method can produce results that are both charming and nostalgic. Compact flowers and flat leaves are the most suitable candidates or generally, any flowers that do not normally have a glossy sheen when fresh. Gently heat the wax, which can be either white or colored, in water. Don't let it boil. Then immerse the flowers head first into the wax. It is often a good idea to tie them with wire beforehand, as they will become heavier with the extra weight of the wax. After immersion, allow to drain and quickly dip them into cold water to make the surfaces glossy. If you repeat the process several times, the flowers will gain a completely airtight wax coating.

BRUSHING

An early method for treating fragile flowers was to brush them with gum arabic – a product used in confectionery-making. Both gum arabic and egg-white (which can also be used together with fine sugar) are excellent preserving agents. Gum arabic is available from druggists and 1oz should be sufficient for an initial trial. Dissolve the gum in twice the quantity of warm water and then gently brush the flowers with the mixture. You may find it easier to wire the flowers beforehand. The complete drying process will take several days in all.

I often dip small flowers into a jar containing the solution. The final effect is very natural.

IMPORTANT GENERAL TIPS

– It is a good idea to try out different preserving methods for different types of flowers.

– I have always found it very useful to record the results of my work in a notebook.

– Dried flowers must be stored in a dark, cool and dry place (a shoe box is ideal).

– As a precaution against vermin, I usually enclose a little dried santolina, wormwood, cedar wood or feverfew.

– Flowers for drying should be dry and picked, preferably, just before midday.

– In fall and winter, collect dry grasses, twigs, leaves and pine cones.

– When preserving flowers, always be prepared for some things to go wrong.

– When flowers start to look unattractive, use them for filling sachets and small cushions, or alternatively gild them with gold or silver paint from an aerosol spray can. Metallic car-paint in spray cans from an auto accessory store also provides a variety of attractive colors.

– Fragile petals and leaves that you do not want to curl up can be individually pressed. You can use a special press or even a telephone directory.

Methods and means	Procedure and timing	Quantity and suitability of materials	Tips
1. Drying flat a) In the home b) In the sun c) In the oven d) In the micro-wave	Loosely scatter the flower heads, petals and leaves a) Up to one week on a large surface b) During the day only, 1 to 2 days c) At 120°F, with ducted air, between 20 minutes and 2 hours (check frequently) d) High watt setting, 5–30 minutes (check)	a) For large quantities b) Only on hot summer days c) Fast, often with good results d) Fast, often with good results	Very suitable for pot pourri
2. Standing a) In a little water b) In glycerine	a) Bunches, individual twigs, with a little water only, up to 2 weeks in a warm place (eg. above the heating) b) One part glycerine (from a druggist) to two parts boiling water. Liquid should reach 2 in up freshly cut stalks	a) Flowers, stems with berries b) Mature foliage (beech, box, mahonia)	For bunches
3. Hanging a) Indoors b) Outdoors	Flowers should be arranged as tied bunches or by varieties and hung upside down in a warm ventilated place.	Good for large quantities b) Only briefly during the day in hot weather otherwise the flowers soon fade.	For bunches
4. Embedding a) In quartz or bird-cage sand b) In borax c) In washing powder d) In silica gel	Plants should be embedded in the preserving material and carefully covered. b–d) Tightly sealed containers are required. a) Easily obtainable, but results variable b) Better in combination with c) washing powder d) Initial outlay high, but can be re-used.	Expensive, but can have particularly attractive results with small items.	For bunches and pot pourri
5. Immersion a) In wax b) In gum arabic	Immerse the flower, allow it to drain and then repeat the process. a) Heat the wax until it liquifies b) Dissolve the powder in twice the quantity of water	Flowers with small heads should be wired beforehand	For bunches and pot pourri
6. Brushing a) With gum arabic b) With egg-white c) With added sugar	Petals are edible, but only within 24 hours and if egg-white is used. a) Use a high, narrow vessel b) Beat 1–2 egg-whites very stiffly c) Sprinkle the brushed petals with fine sugar	These old-fashioned methods usually ensure preservation of both color and form. c) Sugar is also an effective preserving agent and looks attractive on small roses	Particularly for edible decorations

WIRING

TOOLS
Pruning shears for cutting flowers and twigs
Knife for trimming stalks.
Scissors
Tweezers

LENGTHENING OR SUPPORTING
Take a length of supporting wire and bend one end into a firm loop (e). Lay the loop against the stem in such a way that the short end is on the left side of the stem. Your thumb should be pressing on both the stem and the wire.

STEMS AND FLOWERS
With some kinds of flowers, greater stability can be obtained by passing the wire through the bottom of the flower head (g), trailing the short end of the loop down the side of the stem and then winding the long end around the other end of the loop and the stem as a support (h).

FLORISTRY TAPE
To secure stems that have been wired and to improve their appearance, the individual stems can lastly be securely taped (j) with a length of floristry tape. As an alternative, all the stems in the final display can be taped together with floristry tape.

WIRES AND SUPPORTS
Wires come in various lengths and thicknesses. For our purpose, the most important are:
a) Green painted supporting wire
b) Green painted or colored reel wire
c) Decorative wire sleeving
d) Floristry tape

With your other hand, take hold of the long end of the wire loop (better leverage) and wind it tightly around the stem and the short end of the loop (f). The wound end should now lie snugly against the stem.

Here the wire has simply been passed through the base of the flower head and then wound twice round the stem before continuing to run parallel with it (i). In this example, the wire could also be run along the stem and secured with floristry tape.

DECORATIVE WIRE SLEEVING
Slide the decorative wire sleeving over the reel wire or the supporting wire (l). Secure it at the end with a twist or slide it further along as required. You can make either a closed loop (m) or an open loop (n).

CLOVES
Cut 1 in of decorative wire sleeving and 8 in of reel wire. Gently slide the sleeving onto the reel wire in such a way that it sits squarely in the middle. Then bend the wire around the head of the clove in such a way that the clove has a golden collar (o).

CINNAMON STICKS
Bend a length of (green) supporting wire to form a loop and place this over the cinnamon stick or pieces of cinnamon stick (r), so that you can wind the longer end of the loop securely around the shorter end.

STAR ANISE
Two pieces of colored reel wire, about 8 in in length, are arranged across the top of the star anise (t) and then securely twisted together underneath. The ends of the wire should be bound with floristry tape. (This can also be done with mosses and pine cones).
PINE CONES

Although some pine cones do not have stalks, they all have gaps in their structure. A wire loop should be passed through these gaps, preferably at the level of the lower scales (w). For security the wire can be pulled through twice and then directed downward. Arrange the end of the wire so

that it is parallel to the stalk of the clove and then wind the other end of the wire around both (p). Finally, the whole stalk is bound with floristry tape. You can, of course, do the same thing with other round shapes, such as rose hips, acorns or eucalyptus.

If you did not fit a length of decorative sleeving over the visible portion of wire beforehand (s), you should now cover the top piece of wire with an appropriate winding. The stalk should be wound with floristry tape. If a number of cinnamon sticks are to be used together, they should be securely wired at both ends.

LEAVES
Turn the leaf over onto its front, push the wire through the leaf just to the right of the midrib and then bend it back again (u). The lefthand end of the wire should run parallel with the center and the righthand end should be wound around both of these.

DELICATE FLOWERS, BERRY SPRAYS AND GRASSES
First, you will need to make a bunch out of delicate flowers and then wire them together (x). If you are working with sprays of berries, you should secure the bunch directly beneath the berries.

TYING BOUQUETS AND SPRAYS

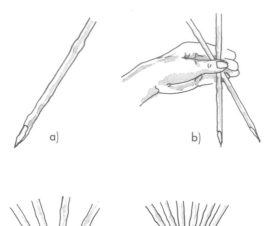

a)

b)

With one hand, grasp the flower, which is slightly angled toward the right, between your thumb, forefinger and middle finger at the point where you intend to make the tie. Then place the second flower across this point in such a way that the petals are to the left and the end of the stalk is to the right (b) of the first flower.

RADIAL BOUQUETS

Firstly, remove all remaining leaves from the bottom third of the stalks (a).

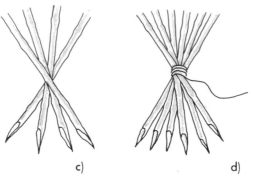

c)

d)

Continue in the same way with the remaining flowers, being careful to ensure that the angle is a little greater each time (c). This will produce a spiral without any cross-overs. Giving a little twist from time to time will give the bouquet a round shape. Continue in this way until the bouquet is ready.

Finally, hold the shorter end of a length of raffia firmly with your thumb and wind the raffia several times around the narrowest part of the bouquet (d). At this point, you can lay the bouquet down and knot the ends of the raffia. The bouquet should be placed in water as quickly as possible.

PARALLEL BOUQUETS

For classical, parallel tied bouquets (such as Victorian posies), you should start in the center and work the materials in a ring around the center (e). For bouquets of herbs, the bunched stalks are normally bound with floristry tape after each ring.

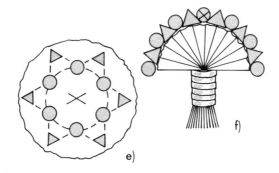

e)

f)

The horizontal bouquet should then be secured and the stalks should be tied with wire (bouquets of herbs) or raffia (posies) (f) and the ends should be knotted. The height of the bouquet will depend upon the point at which the stalks are tied.

DRY ARRANGEMENTS

If you want an arrangement of parallel flowers in a line, you should arrange your dry foam block below the edge of the container (g). Start by inserting a small number of flowers at conspicuous points.

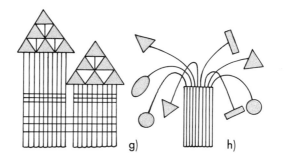

g)

h)

If you want to insert the flowers at an angle, the dry foam block should extend above the rim of the container, but don't forget to round off the edges (h). Start by inserting the flowers in the middle and then the longest to the right and to the left, front and back, and then lastly add the diagonals.

Shapes of Bouquets and Sprays

A semi-circular outline with numerous possibilities of constructing the bouquet depending on the arrangement of the individual component materials: The posy and the "structured" bouquet, with their tightly packed floral coverings, and the round-tied bouquet, with gaps between the individual flowers (a).

For flat-tied bouquets, the outline from above can be circular, but it can be shorter from the front and back and longer from the two sides (b).

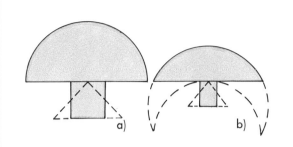

a) b)

The drop or cone shaped outline is often used in "classical" variations (c). Depending on the raw materials used (dry, or possibly fresh flowers in tubes), bouquets can be worked in such a way that they hang at an angle, horizontally or vertically (d).

It is important to note that the outline of a bouquet becomes relatively compact if the flowers are all worked at the same level. This is frequently done by using all large flower heads. Given the availability of different shapes, the larger flower heads are usually arranged in the center, while those with a lighter appearance and the more unusual shapes, are frequently arranged on the outside.

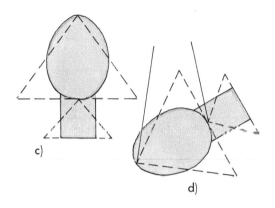

c) d)

The "standing" bouquet is gathered as high up the stems as possible. It usually consists of a single component material (say, corn stalks), but it can also be made of flowers that are curving or trailing in shape and loosely bound together (e).

Bouquets that trail on one, two or all sides are particularly suitable for higher positions, for example on a plinth (f) or in an overhead hanging arrangement.

Parallel arrangements produce a wealth of possible shapes, for example, those having a geometric outline but with a single type of flower, or alternatively with flower stalks forming interesting lines. (See, for example, the "Dry Arrangements" on page 24). Examples of parallel-tied bouquets and sprays can be found on various pages below, including 34, 35, 50, 58 and 74.

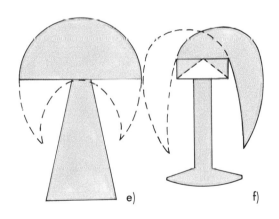

e) f)

Flat bouquets are produced by starting with the longest stems and surrounding these on both sides and above with progressively shorter ones (g).

One variety of a flat, tied bouquet can be seen on page 40, together with an accompanying potpourri (see "Evening fragrances").

g)

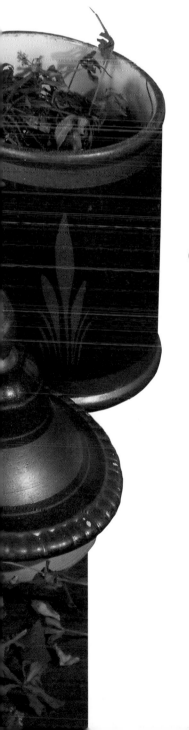

POTPOURRI & POMANDERS

Brighten up your home with your own

creations of fragrant arrangements.

They also make wonderful and original gifts.

POTPOURRI

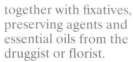

Making potpourri does not take a great deal of time but you will need patience to go through all the stages of preparation.

Firstly, make sure that all parts of the plants that you are using are completely dry. The drying process reduces the volume of the materials by more than half so I recommend that you only use flowers that can be dried easily in large quantities. Depending on the season and the individual fragrances, you can make the potpourri mix with berries and rose-hips, or pine cones, conifer needles and bark – any kind of wood will be an outstanding carrier for fragrances. Also, your favorite bouquets and garden flowers can be a wealth of useful materials once they have started to fade and to dry. Seasonal flowers are a bargain and you can add attractive kitchen spices such as cloves and even powdered herbal teas which often have a deliciously fruity perfume.

When you assemble the ingredients for your potpourri, take care to get a good balance of colors, different structures, textures, and sizes. The dried components will give off only a weak scent, but this can be intensified with the addition of essential oils. You may want to choose a "theme" for your potpourri, such as variations of color; seasons; just flowers; just spices; leaves; plain white or green; woodland; meadows; the Orient or even special scent combinations for an office (to promote concentration), a waiting room (relaxing, refreshing), or a nursery (soothing, cheerful), to mention just a few possibilities. Use your imagination!

Special fixatives which hold or fix the fleeting scents are very important. These should be used in different forms in all potpourri, including various forms of oil and powder (such as cinnamon or orange). A wide range of dried herbs, barks, flowers, roots and resins can be obtained from specialist stores, together with fixatives, preserving agents and essential oils from the druggist or florist.

Adding fixatives gives the matured potpourri a slightly dusty effect, so I usually save my best flowers until the end and add them as a last minute decoration.

And lastly, don't forget that your potpourri won't last for ever. It will remain attractive only for two or three years at the most and the scent will probably disappear completely within six months. There are various precautions you can take to prolong use. One way is to keep your potpourri in a container with a lid – for example in an attractive glass jar – and then to open the lid from time to time so that you can enjoy the fragrance. Or, if you are using an open container, you can prolong the scent by adding a sprinkling of natural essential oils. These will have a beneficial effect on both your physical and your spiritual wellbeing as well as providing a delicious fragrance which can be topped up from time to time.

Shop-bought potpourri, especially the cheaper ones, I'm afraid to say, may contain colored wood shavings that have been sprayed with synthetic perfumes which are either unpleasantly pungent or very short-lived.

Potpourri can be displayed in a variety of ways: boxes, baskets, china and porcelain dishes and plates, glass bowls, in fact anything you have to hand. It is fun, too, to keep your eye open for a container to add to your collection when browsing in antique shops or even a rummage sale.

Match the container to the potpourri; one made from pine needles and cones, citrus peel and country flowers would suit a basket, while one comprising petals from roses, delphiniums and other garden flowers may best complement a porcelain or china bowl.

BASIC RECIPE FOR POTPOURRI

Mix the pulverized fixatives thoroughly with the essential oils. Then very carefully add the mixture to your combination of flowers and herbs and transfer the whole lot into a container with a tightly fitting lid. Your potpourri will then ripen gradually as the fragrant components mingle. Don't forget to give the container a good shake every few days, to make sure that the ingredients are well and truly mixed. After four to six weeks the potpourri will be ready. If you now lift the lid, you will be greeted with a penetrating, and possibly unpleasant, wave of scent. Don't let this worry you. Once the potpourri has been set up in a room, the scent will become stabilized and weaker. Afterwards you will be able to modify the potpourri by putting your own combination of fragrant oils in the respective proportions into a small flask and adding the same quantity of at least one fixative oil, for example tonka bean oil. Then gradually pour this mixture over your potpourri. You should then leave it a little longer in the closed container. The scent given off by the moist potpourri is simply divine.

INGREDIENTS FOR THE BASIC RECIPE

4-8 oz mixed and well dried flowers,
Up to 3 oz dried herbs, such as lavender or balm,
Up to 3 oz of dried spices (many of these, such as cinnamon, nutmeg or star anise, also have a fixative effect
Approx. 2 oz powdered fixative, for example:
1 oz, orris root, and
1 oz benzoin, styrax or cinnamon
At least 30 drops of fragrant oil(s)

"JOIE DE VIVRE" POTPOURRI
(See illustration below)
4 oz rose petals, small rose heads and buds
1 oz woodruff
1 1/2 oz orange peel
1 1/2 oz lavender flowers
1 oz cinnamon sticks
1/2 oz blades of mace
1/2 oz powdered cinnamon
1 oz powdered orris root
10 drops rose oil
10 drops geranium oil
10 drops orange oil

Fragrance note: warm, relaxing, flowery, refreshing

WOODLAND POTPOURRI

4oz pine needles, conifers or evergreen (holly or box tree)
2 oz pine cones, bark, moss, beech-nuts and eucalyptus
$1/2$ oz dried flowers
$1/2$ oz each of allspice, star anise and crushed clove
$1/2$ oz powdered kalmia root
10 drops cedar oil
5 drops of each of the following: pine oil, orange oil, bay oil and patchouli oil.

Fragrance note: Intense, rustic, recommended for colds and chills)

A COLORFUL MEDLEY

4oz assorted flowers
$1/2$ oz each of lavender, mixed fruit, herbs and conifer,
$3/4$ oz coriander and of cinnamon sticks,
1 oz powdered orris root,
10 tonka beans (crushed),
10 drops each of lavender and lilac oil
5 drops each cinnamon and citronella oil

Fragrance note: soft, gentle and relaxing

SPICED POTPOURRI

4 oz spices (nutmeg, cinnamon, clove, star anise, caraway, ginger)
$1/2$ oz each of the following: ground allspice, caraway, nutmeg and cinnamon,
10 drops of bergamot oil,
5 drops each of the following: clove oil, cinnamon oil, coriander oil and Ylang-Ylang oil
2 drops juniper oil

Fragrance note: spicy, strong and warm

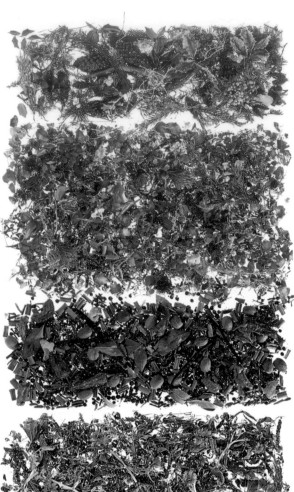

A HERBAL POTPOURRI

4 oz herbs (clary, lavender, balm and mint),
$1/2$ oz mini-sprays of lavender, marigold and nasturtium flowers,(tied with colored raffia)
$1 1/2$ oz powdered orris root,
10 drops bergamot oil
5 drops each of: lemon oil, peppermint oil and clary oil
3 drops each rosemary and verbena oil

Fragrance note: stimulating, spicy and refreshing

A POTPOURRI FOR A NURSERY

$3 1/2$ oz camellia
$1 1/2$ oz cornflower and lavender, mixed
$1 1/2$ oz powdered orris root,
$1 1/2$ oz tonka beans (crushed)
10 drops each lavender and balm oil
5 drops each camellia and tonka oil

Fragrance note: fruity, sweet and cheerful

A REFRESHING POTPOURRI

4oz peel (citrus fruits and apple)
$1/2$ oz each lemon grass and lemon balm
10 apricot or similar pits
2 vanilla pods
$1 1/2$ oz powdered orris root
15 drops lemon grass oil
5 drops lime and grapefruit oil
3 drops tonka oil and orange blossom oil
Fragrance note: fresh and fruity; purifies the air

POMANDERS

PRESERVING COMPOUND
2 oz powdered cinnamon
1½ oz ground cloves,
1½ oz allspice
1½ oz powdered orris root
1 packet of gingerbread spice
20 drops clove oil (optional)
10 drops cinnamon oil
10 drops orange, neroli or lime oil.

For these you need absolutely perfect citrus fruits or apples, together with top quality cloves. First, make the preserving compound (described on the left). The quantities given should be enough for between six and eight pomanders and the compound can be stored in a sealed container until needed again.

Make a number of holes in the fruit at random and press a clove into each hole right up to the head. Children love doing this! Bear in mind, however, that the fruit will shrink a little as it dries, so that the spaces between the cloves will close up. If you do not use enough cloves, there is a risk that the fruit will start to turn moldy. Place one or more pieces of fruit prepared in this manner directly into the spiced compound and also scatter a little on top of the fruit.

During the first fourteen days, you should turn the fruit every day and tap it gently with a spoon to dislodge any remaining powder. During this time, the pomanders should be stored in a closed container. If you want to enhance the scent afterwards, sprinkle the pomander with alcohol and replace it in the compound.

Pomanders give off a fragrance redolent of winter and Christmas but are an ideal decoration for any room throughout the entire year. As well as being ripened in a sealed container, they should spend a further fourteen days lying in a dish containing the spiced compound.

A FESTIVAL

OF
FRAGRANCES

Classical and modern compositions,

arrangements in a multitude of colors

and fragrances for every occasion.

FRAGRANCES ALL YEAR ROUND

THE MAGIC OF MAY

Fragrance note: aromatic, spicy. Rich in floral perfumes with a hint of lemon.

A beautiful posy of old-fashioned flowers to bring back memories of childhood days. Fragrant lilies of the valley, warm, spicy lilac and bittersweet elderflower are further enriched by the lemon-scented leaves of pelargonium and aromatic herbs, such as ginger, sage and lavender – truly magnificent. The rounded form of the bouquet is emphasized by the use of a fabric sleeve.

PERFECT SPLENDOR

Fresh figs, violet pastilles, dried rhododendron and other flowers, together with a nostalgic Christmas tree bauble.

Fragrance note: Full, rich and sweet with an underlying spicy and aromatic flavor.

In the weeks between spring and summer, nature gives us a wealth of strong and headily scented flowers.

This time of the year is visually brilliant with "older" varieties of peonies, roses, elderflower, stock and flowering clematis. This loose yet full bouquet displays a purposefully irregular distribution of shades of purple and red.

The arrangement is accompanied by an appetizing display on an etagere and by a sachet of lavender – a modern, romantic still life.

VARIATIONS ON POSY STYLES

Fragrance note: Warm and spicy (posy on the right) Light, sweet and intense (middle) Soft and gentle with a hint of freshness (left) – clearly defined fragrances.

Plain and simple posies made of pinks, lilies of the valley, wallflowers and guelder roses, have their own individual warm and spicy perfumes. The "Safari" (**right**) pink posy illustrated above has a perfume of nutmeg and cinnamon.

Apart from the use of conventional frills, there are many other ways of presenting bouquets, such as holders or velvet ribbons, watered silk or silk paper, or finely woven green shoots – let your imagination run riot. The above photograph illustrates three possibilities, in which the simple form of the bouquet matches the discreet colors and unassuming character of the flowers.

Attractive and seasonally decorative posies can also be created from dried and wire-stemmed seed heads, small pine cones, nutmegs, Christmas baubles, in fact anything you choose and which will combine to make a pleasing effect. (See page 74)

The charm of this composition (**above**) is in its simplicity and clean lines – a surface in gleaming marble; the tall, glass candleholder with the plain white candle and the translucent glass ball.

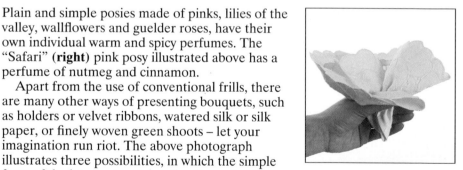

How to make a frill for the pink posy.

The gentle mauve violets add a slight shading of color to a vase of mixed woodland greenery, which includes leaves of the wild strawberry plant.

One day in spring, I was out picking flowers when my little daughter, said: "It's so cold, the flowers should have coats". And so I acted on her advice and "covered" them with transparent colored glass.

The combination of meadow flowers and large glass vases may seem a little strange but you will see from the charming visual effect that you don't always have to use china or earthenware vases.

There are three bunches simply because the flowers were all of different lengths and appearance. To prevent upstaging any of them, I divided them into three groups and arranged them in separate containers. Now I can really enjoy the first, fragrant breaths of spring.

All flowers for each arrangement should be cut first to the same length before being finally trimmed and transferred to a vase. Violets can be added to the final displays.

A BREATH OF SPRING

Fragrance note: Discreetly sweet, gentle and soft (right), honey sweet (center), musty-damp (left) – just like a spring meadow!

37

(Roses, roses and more roses –
see illustration on page 32/33)

ROSES, ROSES AND MORE ROSES (BOUQUET)

Ingredients: approx. 20 roses, 2 bunches of lavender, watered silk and holder, ribbon, raffia, a triangular paper cornet, plastic beaker, wet foam block, mounting pins.

Preparation: Cut the roses and place them in water, soak a suitable quantity of foam block.

Method: Cut off the tip from the paper cornet, crimp the top of the plastic beaker and put in the soaked foam block so that it projects over the top of the beaker. Then insert the roses firmly, making a perfect semicircle. Lavender sprays can be tucked between the roses. The stems must be deep and firm. Finally, wrap the silk around the cornet and secure with pins. Embellish the final arrangement with a decorative ribbon.

Tip: The bouquet can also be tied with the stems upright and arranged in close sequence.

THE MAGIC OF MAY

Ingredients: Roses, elderflowers, lilies of the valley, lavender, sage, scented-leaved pelargonium, lilac, ginger, dried leaves, a strong piece of cloth, wire and raffia.

Preparation: Prepare the flowers, wire the ginger and the dried leaves (pages 22/23).

Method: Cut out three strips of cloth, gather them to form a fan and then wire them (a). For the bouquet, hold the roses in such a way that the length of stalk above your hand determines the size of the resulting semicircle (the longer the stems, the larger the bouquet). Working from the center (see the Chapter entitled "Tying Bouquets and Sprays" on page 24), make either a spiral (i.e. radial) or a parallel tie for the bouquet. This arrangement always includes several flowers of the same type. Finally, arrange the three fans like a sleeve around the bouquet and tie together.

(The Magic of May – see
illustration on page 34)

Fragrance note: Sweet and gentle rose scent, with a hint of lavender. For the rose potpourri: sweet, charming and soft.

INGREDIENTS FOR THE
ROSE POTPOURRI
4 oz dried flowers, such as roses, lavender, maize or myrtle
1/2 oz each cloves, star anise and cinnamon sticks
1 oz each powdered cinnamon and orris root
15 drops rose oil
3 drops each myrtle, lavender, orange and cinnamon oil.

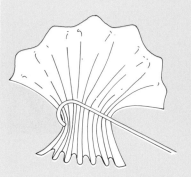

a) Gather the cloth strips into a fan and then wire.

PERFECT SPLENDOR

Ingredients: Elderflowers, lilac, stock, fragrant roses (I have used "Jacaranda" and "Sterling Silver" in this arrangement), peonies, sage, blooming clematis and a piece of chiffon cloth in a color that matches or contrasts with your flowers.

Preparation: Remove all the leaves from the elderflowers and lilac and with the other flowers, make sure that none of the leaves are immersed in the water to avoid risk of rotting.

Method: Firstly, bend any of the stems that are still straight and arrange the elderflower, lilac and stock stems in the vase. Then add the larger flowers. Finally, insert the clematis and sage into any gaps.

Tip: Cut the stems first before arranging the flowers.

(Perfect Splendor – see illustration on page 35)

VARIATIONS ON POSY STYLES

Ingredients: *Right-hand posy:* "Safari" pinks, decorative strips, frill. *Center posy:* Hydrangea, lilies of the valley (with leaves). *Left-hand posy:* 1 rose, wallflowers, guelder roses, wide-mesh lace frill, wide decorative band with frill strip.

Preparation: Wire the loops.

Method: *Right-hand posy:* Holding the frill firmly (page 36) in one hand, add the pinks and decorative strips, tie. *Center posy:* Place the lilies of the valley both inside and also around the semicircle of hydrangea (a). Form the frill from hydrangea leaves of the same size, and tie. *Left-hand posy:* Draw the rose down through the center of the lace frill, so it looks as if it is wearing a ruff. Then make three rings in succession, the first with the wallflower, the second with the guelder rose and the third with the wired band. Finally, tie with numerous windings of the decorative strip.

(Variations on the posy styles – see illustration on page 36)

a) Arrange the lilies of the valley both inside and around the hydrangea.

A BREATH OF SPRING

Ingredients: A selection of wild flowers and violets.

Method: Cut each flower type to roughly the same length, put together and arrange. Place the bunch of violets in a very small amount of water.

(A Breath of Spring – see illustration on page 37)

EVENING
FRAGRANCES

Fragrance note: Alluring,
delightful, spicy and fresh

This attractive bouquet invites leisurely contemplation.

One evening, after a long and hectic day, I wandered idly around my garden, enjoying the delicious potpourri of perfumes in the air. Sweet honeysuckle, pungent mint and rosy-pink kalmia – they all inspired me to start collecting a bunch of flowers and herbs whose scent is particularly delicious in the evening.

When I tied my bouquet I ensured that each flower was shown to its best advantage. The gems in my arrangement are new and old-fashioned roses which add both grace and beauty as well as perfume.

Fragrance note: Gentle rose perfume with a warm and spicy undercurrent and a breath of orange – a sweet, but by no means sugary, bouquet.

This traditional rose potpourri is characterized by a multitude of exotic spices and an orange pomander.

A Cheerful Spray

This light, sweet-smelling early summer arrangement features camellia, vetch and other small flowers, including the gentle sweet pea and varieties of light, graceful flowers, which appear to be rising out of the chunkier elements of the bouquet. Luxuriant peonies, achillea and the other larger flowers all complement the large-bellied copper vase to create a beautifully balanced effect.

Fragrance note: Bouquet – gentle and hovering, sweet and spicy. Potpourri – piquant, fresh and flowery.

This beautiful potpourri container with its perforated lid contains an enticingly fragrant mixture of moist flowers.

Fragrance note: Bouquet – Tangy and spicy, yet intensely sweet. Potpourri – lemon fresh and piquant. Particularly good against pests and as an air freshener.

These carnations seem to be doing a balancing act all by themselves in the vase and the lilies in the potpourri look incredibly fresh? This still life with its clear colors and shapes is full of surprises. How does it work?

The carnations and the lily in the champagne bucket are mounted on concealed pinholders and the flowers in the dish are arranged in tubes filled with water. The glass vessel contains a potpourri (see also page 30 – "A Spiced Potpourri").

RUSTIC SILVER

Although the candle-holders and the dish appear to be made of silver, they are in fact made of metallized glass.

43

A Basket of Fragrance

Here is a medley of tangy garden herbs, which instead of being a delight for the palate, have become a real feast for the eyes. The plant material: a multitude of kitchen herbs, such as flowering sage, peppermint, lavender and oregano and an accompaniment of roses.

On this page and the next are two alternative ways of arranging and displaying the same ingredients. In one, the basket is soft and the contents seem to pour out of it, while in the other, the arrangement is much more upright and close-knit. Even when the flowers and herbs have dried, they still look just as appetizing.

Fragrance note: Strong, spicy perfume mingling with the sweet scent of roses

44

When planning displays and bouquets it is important to work out in advance your proposed outline and how to position and arrange the respective flowers (here they are curved and the longer ones are on the outside).

You will find that you can control and experiment with shades of color.

(Evening Fragrances – Bouquet;
See illustration on pages 40/41)

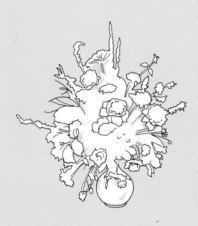

(A Cheerful Spray - see illustration
on page 42)

EVENING FRAGRANCES (BOUQUET)

Ingredients: A variety of herbs and flowers including peppermint, lemon balm, honeysuckle, phlox, roses, sage, and sweet scabious. Raffia.

Preparation: Tidy and trim at least the bottom quarter of the stems.

Method: Always start with the longest flowers and then add the shorter ones, using as many as possible with curved stems. During the tying process, I try to include a number of smaller formations, so that the longer ingredients can "hang" freely.

The adjacent list of ingredients for the "Evening Fragrance" potpourri should be worked in the same way as the Basic Recipe for Potpourri shown on page 29.

A CHEERFUL SPRAY

Ingredients: Garden flowers such as achillea, camellias, roses, sweet peas and common jasmine

Preparation: Clean and cut the stems, place them in water.

Method: Using the larger flowers, construct the general shape of the spray. Important: use as many flowers with curved stems as possible, otherwise your spray will look a little too stiff.

BASIC RECIPE FOR A MOIST POTPOURRI

Ingredients: 8 oz strongly perfumed flowers, 3 oz fixative, prepared from ground spices and roots, 40 drops of a suitable fragrant oil, kitchen salt, and brown sugar.

Method: Leave the flowers to dry for about 2 days. Then pour them into a dish and cover with salt (1 cup of salt to 3 cups of flowers). Weight this down with a plate and a large stone. You can repeat this step as often as you like (a). Every third day drain off the fluid that has accumulated. Stir and add a sprinkling of sugar. After 2 months at the most, the crumbly mass should be combined – as with the dry potpourri – with fixatives and oils. It should then be sealed and left to mature for 5 weeks.

INGREDIENTS FOR THE
"EVENING FRAGRANCE"
POTPOURRI
4 oz elderflowers, roses, apple peel and lavender
1¹/₂ oz mixed cinnamon sticks, mace, cloves and star anise
1¹/₂ oz powdered orris root
8 drops each rose oil, rosewood oil, bergamot oil and cinnamon oil.

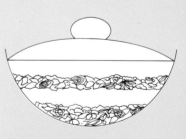

a) The moist potpourri is arranged in layers: 3 parts flowers to 1 part of salt and then weighted with a plate and a stone in a container.

POTPOURRI INGREDIENTS
RUSTIC SILVER (DISH)
4 oz dried flowers, such as, roses, achillea, gypsophila
the zest of 5 to 10 lemons (not sprayed)
1 oz lemon grass
3/4 oz cloves
1 oz powdered orris root
20 drops lemon grass oil
10 drops bergamot oil.

RUSTIC SILVER (BOUQUET)
Ingredients: Carnations (10 to 20), regal lilies, a madonna lily, 2 pinholders, sand, elastic band.
Preparation: Remove the leaves from the lower part of the stem, cut and secure the carnations 2 in above the cut with the elastic band.
Method: Place the larger of the two pinholders in the center of the vase for the carnations. Then tie the carnations and arrange them on the pinholder. Place the lily alongside. Then add the sand if necessary to stabilize the arrangement. Decorate the carnations with a gaily colored cord or band tied loosely around the top of the stem. For the potpourri dish, work the ingredients on the left as for the Basic Recipe for Potpourri on page 29.

(Rustic Silver – see illustration on page 43)

A BASKET OF FRAGRANCE I
Ingredients: Garden herbs and roses, a basket with foil or a mounting dish, wet foam block.
Preparation: Cut the foam block to size and soak.
Method: As the flowers come out of the basket at an angle, the wet foam must be higher than the edge of the dish (a). Firstly, sketch out the general shape that you want to create. It is very important here to use curving flowers.

(A Basket of Fragrance I – see illustration on page 44)

A BASKET OF FRAGRANCE II
Ingredients: Garden herbs, roses, basket with foil or a watertight vessel, wet foam block.
Preparation: Cut the foam block to size and soak.
Method: Define the general shape of your arrangement by inserting the flowers, with the longest at each end, into the foam block. (b). Vary the flowers to make it more natural. Then arrange the roses on the basis of color.
Tip: With tall vessels, there is no need for foam block. Arrange the flowers with their stems parallel and secure with raffia or a decorative cord.

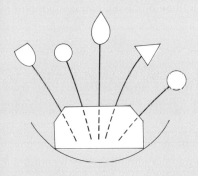

a) Round off the edges of the wet foam block (above the edge of the dish).

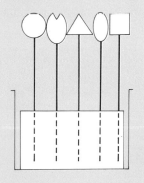

b) Wet foam block (below the edge of the vessel).

(A Basket of Fragrance II – see illustration on page 45)

THE
SLEEPING
BEAUTY

An " Alice in Wonderland" world,
in which a standing arrangement of
rose stems towers over items of
furniture borrowed from a doll's
house. The combination of
impenetrable thorns and sweet-
smelling scent reminds me of the
fairytale "The Sleeping Beauty."

Why not experiment yourself
by interpreting some of the well-
known fairytales? You will find it is
an absorbing pastime. These
subjects are often used in flower-
arranging competitions.

Fragrance note: Warm and
festive (potpourri) accompanied
by a hint of amber

The rose theme of this arrangement makes the most of the way rose-hip branches hang loosely but powerfully, emphasized even further by the reversed proportions. The arrangement is accompanied by sweetly fragrant roses, with stems placed in tubes filled with water and wrapped in moss. The rose-hips and flowers will gradually dry out, but you will be able to replace the flowers as you wish.

Later, you can add white Christmas roses (with water-filled tubes) to make an attractive pre-Christmas decoration.

This standing arrangement will look just as appealing outside your front door as in your living-room. But if you do not have the space indoors (the height of the arrangement is 58 in) you can always make a smaller version.

The rose theme is continued on all three levels of the antique rose stand. On the top level, there is a gilded, waxed rose lying next to a rose pomander. The middle level is dominated by a rose-hip pomander, while on the bottom level there is a porous pottery container with a moist potpourri, giving off a beautiful scent of . . . . roses!

SHADES OF FALL

This display evokes memories of cool but sunny fall days, rustling foliage and magnificent colors. This is the time of mellow fruit and abundance. Once again, nature reveals her extravagant beauty and collecting these seasonal treasures is a joy in itself.

I have created an idyllic still life composition by simply binding and displaying the different items. The plant material is enhanced by perfumes provided by the warm and woody cedar bundle, the pungent spray of lavender, scented sachets and cinnamon sticks in conjunction with the spicy potpourri. The fragrance is increased by dried sunflowers, plums and chestnuts that are concealed in the basket.

Fragrance note: Like an autumn walk, with spicy and refreshing accents

Fragrance note: Fresh and spicy with the distinctive scents of eucalyptus and lemon.

"WAX" FLOWERS

An expressive pottery container is a real eye-catcher. The ones I used here are simple in appearance, but very individual. The perfectly shaped vase matches the shape of the bunch of flowers exactly and the flat dish with slotted lid would be an ideal receptacle for fermented potpourri.

In the long fall and winter months, when the perfume of flowers no longer fills the air, you will have to resort to sweet smelling, imported flowers. The above illustration shows two of these, eucalyptus and "wax flowers", or hoya *carnosa,* which give off a fresh lemon scent when their leaves are bruised.

You can also enrich your combination of perfumes by using fragrant oils in the aroma lamp.

TRANSPORTS OF FRAGRANCE

Bouvardia *longiflora* has an almost magical intensely sweet smell and I was able to combine it successfully with some cooling green plants from around the garden pond – a handful of long grass and a handful of lemon-scented pelargonium leaves. This produced an ensemble with the interesting combination of a heady sweet perfume in contrast to the simple and clear visual effect.

It is fun, too, to play about with the various constituents of your arrangement to see how a simple adjustment can alter the whole balance.

Fragrance note: temptingly sweet and fresh

A BASKET OF SPICES

Fill the tubes (available from your local floral specialist) with water, secure cap and bind with moss and decorative wire.

There is a quiet air of magic about this Christmassy, spicy arrangement with its gentle interplay of colours and its single basket filled with a spicy potpourri.

Cymbidium "Christmas Angel" flowers set in water-filled tubes and fresh green moss are all in keeping with the seasonally traditional nuts, pine cones and cinnamon sticks. Broom, tied with decorative wire and vine shoots round off the effect.

This is an unobtrusive composition, exuding a warm and spicy aroma of tonka, cinnamon and mountain pine (in the potpourri). You can almost hear those Christmas bells!

Fragrance note: warm, with traces of woodland and cinnamon

(The Sleeping Beauty – see illustration on pages 48/49)

THE SLEEPING BEAUTY (BOUQUET)

Ingredients: Rose-hip branches, roses, hops, virgin's bower, moss-wrapped water tubes, decorative wire, a length of stout wire, raffia and protective gloves.

Preparation: Fill the tubes with water and seal.

Method: Firstly, put on your protective gloves! Then stand the first rose-hip branch upright on the ground and arrange the other branches at an angle around this in such a way that all the stems stand up. An arrangement of this size is best tackled by two people together. Firmly secure the bunch with stout wire and cover it with raffia or string. Then secure the water-filled tubes to the branches, taking care that the open ends do not point downward, and insert the roses. Lastly, once you have removed the leaves from the hop tendrils, wind them around the branches and, if necessary, add another couple of bunches of virgin's bower.

Potpourri: Ingredients and instructions as in the Basic Recipe on page 29 (oils: 10 drops rosewood oil, 15 of bay and cinnamon oil).

SHADES OF FALL (BOUQUET)

Ingredients: Autumn flowers (such as asters, dahlias), lavender, cedar wood, cinnamon sticks.

Preparation: Clean and trim stems.

Method: Hold the flowers with their stems upright and parallel and secure tightly just below the flower heads. When the bunch is large enough, tie the bouquet by winding the raffia around the bunch above the level of your fingers. Cut each stem obliquely and to the same length. Finally, place them on a dish filled with water. The lavender is tied in the same way.

Potpourri: Work the ingredients shown for the Shades of Fall Potpourri as described in the Basic Recipe for potpourri on page 29.

(Shades of Fall – see illustration on page 50)

THE SLEEPING BEAUTY POMANDER
Ingredients: 60-80 rose heads
1 dry foam ball (rose pomander)
About 4 handfuls of firm rose-hips
1 dry foam ball (rose-hip pomander)

Method: remove all stems and glue the rose heads and rose-hips closely together onto the dry foam balls with a glue gun.

SHADES OF FALL POTPOURRI
(Comforting against colds and chills)
Ingredients: 4 oz moss, berries, bark, leaves and other sundries, together with strawflowers, sunflowers, dried plums and eucalyptus pods
1 oz star anise
1 $\frac{1}{2}$ oz powdered orris root
10 drops cypress oil and "fresh leaves" perfumed oil
5 drops each bergamot and eucalyptus oils

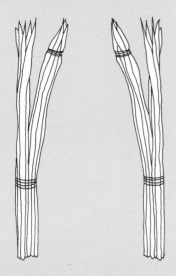

"Wax" Flower – see illustration on page 51)

WAX FLOWERS
Ingredients: Wax flowers (Hoya *carnosa*), eucalyptus pods.
Preparation: Clean stems.
Method: Tie the bouquet in a radial manner. To prevent it from looking monotonous, use either different quantities of the two ingredients, or alternatively just the one ingredient, which will then stand out in splendor against its background. (See page 46 for Moist Potpourri).

TRANSPORTS OF FRAGRANCE
Ingredients: Bouvardia *longiflora,* grasses, lemon-scented pelargonium, white roses, wet foam block, white cord, preserving agent.
Preparation: Cut a slice of wet foam 1¹/₂ in thick and soak.
Method: Remove the bouvardia leaves from the lower part of the stem, cut the flowers and immerse them immediately in warm water (containing a preserving agent), as they are susceptible to water loss.
The leaves of the lemon-scented pelargonium are then arranged flat in layers across the wet foam slice and on top of this is inserted a branch of any softly flowing plant. The two bunches of grasses are firstly tied quite normally as single bunches and then the tops are tied together (a). While doing this, a few blades of grass should be left untied in each bunch. The untied blades from the rear bundle are then tied in with the tied ends of the front bundle and the untied ends from the front bundle are tied in with the tied ends of the rear bundle (b).

(Transports of Fragrance – see illustration on page 52)

A BASKET OF SPICES
Ingredients: A "festive potpourri", nuts, pine cones, cinnamon sticks, broom branches, dried vine shoots, cymbidium flowers, water-filled tubes, moss, decorative wire, Christmas accessories, material.
Preparation: Fill the tubes with water and wrap with moss.
Method: Line the basket with an appropriate cloth or similar material, add the potpourri (see page 29 for the instructions for the Basic Recipe), insert the cymbidium flowers into the water-filled tubes and arrange the accessories to your liking.

INGREDIENTS FOR A FESTIVE POTPOURRI
4 oz. pine and conifer cones
1¹/₂ oz. each of cloves, star anise and cinnamon
1 oz. of powdered orris root
¹/₂ oz. each of clove pepper and ground allspice.
10 drops each of mountain pine, cinnamon and tonka oil.

(A Basket of Spices – see illustration on page 53)

ROMANTIC STILL LIFE

This may be a bouquet of dried flowers, but it has a luxuriant and effusive effect which can be amazing!

In this arrangement, I have used my favorite flowers together with other plants, such as rose-hips and branches of broom to create a large and gentle still life that, instead of having a "dusty" appearance, seems to be full of life. And what is more surprising – that's exactly how it smells!

Fragrance note: Warm and gentle, with a hint of cinnamon.

THE FRAGRANCE OF DRIED BOUQUETS

Gentle perfumes invite relaxation. Perhaps surprisingly their source is a fragrant bouquet made up out of dried geraniums, lavender and rosewood. Fragrance and dried flowers are not generally associated with each other. You can read below how the bouquets can be individually scented.

On this page you will see five varieties of dried bouquets – a bare minimum from a wealth of possibilities. In the three largest of these, the clearly defined outlines radiate such peace and harmony that when it comes to the fine detail, such a variety ensures that the bouquet never becomes boring – in fact the longer you look, the more you see!

Fragrance note: Variable (here a relaxing living room fragrance).

Incidentally: A small bouquet with flowers that have not been artificially colored will continue to delight you for at least 6 months and maybe as much as a year. After that, the colors will be so pale that you will have to start thinking of a new arrangement.

DISPLAYING TYING AND BUNDLING

This decorative still life with its soft and nostalgic presentation contains a rare gem: 20 vanilla pods. As I am very fond of redecorating displays of everlasting flowers, I put the bundle of dried sweetcorn leaves and vanilla pods on its own next to a candle-holder, or alternatively I place a flat bouquet on a fruit bowl on the sideboard. The sun-shaped mirror, with its bundles of hay and their sprinkling of golden glitter, will sometimes grace the table and sometimes the bathroom window-sill.

Caption: The vanilla pods are a visual delight in themselves. In combination with dried sweetcorn leaves, they look for all the world like a swathed jewel.

Fragrance note: Bouquets and orchid flowers can be scented as you wish (here the scent is a mixture of orchid with lotus and tonka).
White bouquet: vanilla and honey.
Red bouquet (above): rose, cinnamon and bay oil (amber scented)
Bundle of hay: freshly cut grass.
Myrtle spray (below): lavender and rose.

59

FRAGRANCE FROM THE AIR

This large, horizontally tied "trailing bouquet" would, without doubt, make a striking feature. The basic structure is formed from strong plastic tubes and wooden spars, around which rose-hip branches, beans, hops and other climbing plants are wound.

No attempt has been made to conceal the connecting points of the tubes, the branches and the tendrils, and these are visually emphasized in a most colorful manner by the use of gaily colored wool or wire. Apart from its unusual construction and its elevated position, the hanging bouquet has a further surprise: the use of water-filled tubes means that the roses can give off fresh, sweet-smelling perfume. They can be replaced by any other kind of flower as the season changes.

The fragrant leaves, flowers and spices knotted to the structure are a source of additional fragrance.

Fragrance note: Gently appealing, sweet, aromatic and spicy.

This original design for a bag of fragrance is shaped like an old-fashioned candy bag and is decorated with fragrant spices such as vanilla pods, cinnamon sticks and dried orange peel, all attached by wire. It makes an unusual wall decoration. Every breath of wind will set the components in movement, so that the vanilla, the cinnamon and the orange will all take turns to dominate.

You can fill the bag with a spicy potpourri of your choice.

An Original Bag of Fragrance

Fragrance note: Spicy and fruity, vanilla, cinnamon and orange.

(Romantic Still Life – see illustration on pages 56/57)

(The Fragrance of Dried Bouquets – see illustration on page 58)

ROMANTIC STILL LIFE

Ingredients: Dried flowers in a range of colors, dry foam block, wire and wool.

Preparation: Secure the dry foam block in the container (if necessary using stones at the sides). Round off any edges that project above the rim of the vessel.

Method: With such a large bouquet, I would recommend that you do not tie it but insert each flower individually. Start with the tallest erect flower and then continue arranging on both the left and the right sides in a horizontal and then in a diagonal line (and also to the back and the front). Use different flowers, otherwise the overall effect will be too monotonous and rigid. Finally, complete the general outline, taking care that the individual flowers are not too close together and that in every case, they have charming neighbors in shape, color and surface textures.

THE FRAGRANCE OF DRIED BOUQUETS

Ingredients: A wide variety of dried flowers and fruit, pine cones, grasses, herbs, decorative band, wire, dry block foam.

Method: All bouquets can be tied with their stems parallel if the fragile flowers are cut just below the heads and wired. However, it is both quicker and easier to insert the stems of a bouquet directly into a dry foam block, or even into a wet foam block, provided that it has not been soaked. Both small bouquets have been tied. For the three larger bouquets, start in each case in the center and insert the flowers in circles around (following the required outline) working outward; lastly add the frills. For the bouquet on the right at the back, the technique of preparing the frill is described on page 38. For the bouquet on the left, proceed as follows: wire a sufficiently wide piece of decorative band in four to six places (see also pages 22/23) and then arrange the wires with the band in the form of a tight circle around the bouquet.

THE FRAGRANCE TRICK:
Mix two fixing oils (here cinnamon and tonka) with a flower oil of your choice (here geranium) in a proportion of 1:1:2. Sprinkle between 10 and 20 drops in each case over the pine cones, the bark and the velvety or "hairy" flowers and then enclose in a sealed container and leave for 4 weeks. Every 2 or 3 weeks add a few drops of the oil to the mixture. Incidentally, flowers with stems will also increase the emission of scent if they are included in a maturing potpourri.

(Displaying, Tying and Bundling – see illustration on page 59)

(Displaying, Tying and Bundling – see illustration on page 59)

ADDING SCENT TO DISPLAYED, TIED AND BUNDLED ITEMS:

Rub a number of cinnamon sticks with cinnamon oil and the dried sweetcorn leaves with vanilla oil. Add fragrance to the bouquets (as described on page 62), sprinkling the bottom bouquet when finished with 5 drops of rose oil, 5 drops of myrtle oil and 5 drops of lavender oil (myrtle oil has a fixative effect).

I also sprinkled 10 drops of hay oil over the bundles of hay and 5 drops of lotus oil mixed with 3 drops of tonka oil to the center of the single flower. The white spray lay in a nursery potpourri (vanilla and honey), and a number of flowers from the top bouquet lay for 4 weeks in a mixture of 10 drops of rose oil, 10 drops of cinnamon oil and 10 drops of bay oil.

ASSEMBLING THE VANILLA BUNDLE:

Arrange the decorative bands firstly crosswise upwards, and then crosswise downwards over the bundle. Finally, knot together.

DISPLAYING, TYING AND BUNDLING

Ingredients: Cinnamon, vanilla, dried sweetcorn leaves, dried flowers, hay, a single flower head dried in silica gel, various decorative bands and wires, golden glitter.

Method: For the bouquets, only the initial flowers should be long and the subsequent flowers (on top in the arrangement) should be shorter, so that the bouquets become layered and are flat at the back. The bundles of hay on the mirror are loosely girdled with the decorative wire and arranged in shape. I have also scattered a little golden glitter over them and added the flower head.

FRAGRANCE FROM THE AIR

Materials: 3 strong plastic tubes, sturdy wooden spars or large cinnamon sticks, rose-hip branches, beans, hops or other climbers, fresh roses, cord, colored wire (or strong wool), 5 water tubes wrapped in moss, nylon thread.

Method: Firstly attach the three plastic tubes to each other, and then attach the spars or the sticks with cord to the plastic tubes to create a basic structure. Secure the rose-hip branches and the climbers to different points on this structure, using colored wire or wool. Arrange the water tubes in such a way that the openings are pointing obliquely upward and insert the fresh roses into the tubes. Use a long length of knotted nylon thread to suspend this trailing bouquet from four prominent points.

AN ORIGINAL BAG OF FRAGRANCE

Ingredients: Strong wrapping paper, glue, wool, wire, 30 to 40 spices in different lengths (such as vanilla pods or cinnamon sticks), spicy potpourri.

Method: Roll up the wrapping paper to form a paper cone and glue. Fill with potpourri. Cut varying lengths of wool in proportion to the size of the paper cone. Tie the spices firmly to each end of the strands. Take a piece of wire and secure it around the middle of the bundle of strands so that they hang down on either side. Now attach the bundle to the top of the cone.

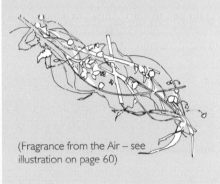

(Fragrance from the Air – see illustration on page 60)

(An Original Bag of Fragrance – see illustration on page 61)

SACHETS, CUSHIONS, PILLOWS AND FRAGRANT PARCELS

It would take a whole book to describe all the different types of relaxing, stimulating, exciting and sweet-smelling types of fragrances – not to mention the wide variety of places in which these can be concealed.

Just take a look around your home and I am sure you will realize how many possible hiding places there could be for hidden scents. The folds of your drapes, for example, could contain refreshing and relaxing sachets and you could keep any number of lemon-scented or moth-repellant sachets among your clothes. You can also have sleep-promoting pillows, filled with hops, balm and lavender. Do you prefer sensuous perfumes in the form of flowers? Bathroom parcels made of tulle, kitchen tiles with a hint of lemon, happy nursery motifs, rustic, romantic or elegant cushions or other creations for your bedroom or living room – here you will find a wealth of ideas, both for yourself and for others. As well as the sachets and cushions that need sewing there are many alternative suggestions if you don't like or don't have time to sew.

Fragrance note: You can choose between sleep-promoting, sensuous, relaxing, refreshing or anything else.

A SPIRAL OF SUNSHINE

In the early part of the summer, meadows are always full of ox-eye daisies and I recently had a marvellous time picking them and playing the old game (do you remember?) . . . "He loves me, he loves me not . . ."

In the end, I had a large amount of dried, white daisy petals and a number of golden sun-shaped centers. Using the round centers of the flowers, and starting with the largest and working down in size, I made this spiral.

Fragrant note: Clear, fresh and crisp

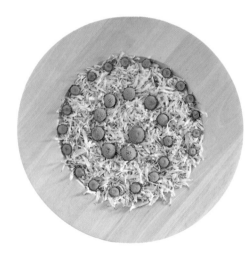

This, and also the following pot-pourri, give a brief indication of the many possible creations you can make with dried flowers, herbs and spices – quite apart from the numerous variations of scents.

HARMONY IN WHITE

This mixture of flowers and spices gives off an elegant, flowery perfume as the look of it might suggest. I like to make up potpourri around the theme of a single color with many different nuances and structures. In this case, the theme is white, with varying shades in flowers of different sizes, and in transparent, smooth and rough petals, sliding gently into cream with a hint of yellow and accompanied by green rose leaves. The white is further emphasized by the discreet arrangement of contrasting black vanilla pods and the background. This potpourri is the essence of discretion in both color and perfume and is ideal for living rooms in particular.

Fragrance note: Elegant, soft with a flowery freshness.

Flowers of every season, lilies of the valley and roses, elderflowers and strawflowers all mingle to create a gentle, discreet composition with a friendly and relaxing perfume.

FLAVORS OF THE ORIENT

This potpourri with its oriental inspiration is warm, cheerful, luxuriant and sensuous. Let yourself be tempted to a relaxing hour or so.

Peony and rose flowers, alder cones, two heads of hops (not enough, of course, to make you feel sleepy), sage and mint have all been arranged with a bundle of long cinnamon sticks on a traditional silver-gray Turkish dining plate.

Next to that, dried apple peel and prickly sweet and dry elderflower make an attractive composition with a contrasting range of colors and surface qualities. Red-cheeked apples and a spicily scented chain of eucalyptus flowers are a promise of further sensuous pleasures.

Fragrance note: Alluring, sensuous and bewitching.

Fragrance note: Intensely exotic and heavy.

Numerous exotic spices, sandalwood and heavily perfumed flowers produce the scent of this exotic potpourri. The other constituents in the arrangement also reveal characteristics of the Far East.

EXOTIC AND FARAWAY PLACES

Bouquet: A bamboo pole was cut into lengths in such a way that each piece was closed at one end and could be filled with water. The pieces of bamboo were then tied together and the flowers were inserted. This means that, depending on how you see it, you have a display of flowers without wet foam, or else a bouquet with its own "built-in reservoir".

Potpourri: Cedar wood and sandalwood, quassia and chili, mace and cardamom, together with other spices and varieties of wood, are all arranged on a wooden platter. The cinnamon sticks look like chopsticks – the vanilla, ginger and paprika, together with the rhododendron flower that has been dried in silica gel, all contribute to the final structure of the arrangement.

(Sachets, Cushions, Pillows and Fragrant Parcels – see illustration on page 64/65)

SCENTED SACHETS AND HEARTS

Filling I: (useful against vermin)
2¹/₂ oz cedarwood shavings
2¹/₂ oz lavender
1¹/₂ oz powdered kalmia root
10 drops of cedarwood oil
OR
15 drops of lavender oil
5 drops of orange oil

Filling II: (invigorating effect)
4 oz lavender flowers, mixed with
1¹/₂ oz powdered orris root, and
a) 15 drops of bergamot oil, 10 drops of grapefruit oil, and 5 drops of lavender oil

OR: (relaxing and soothing effect)
b) 15 drops of geranium oil, and 5 drops each of the following oils: rose, cinnamon and lavender

OR: (increased concentration)
c) 9 drops of hyssop oil, and 5 drops each of the following oils: clary, balm, lemon and juniper

SACHETS, CUSHIONS, PILLOWS AND FRAGRANT PARCELS

For larger items, up to half of the ingredients (lavender, hops, rose petals and the like) can be replaced by oatmeal or fine, completely dry wood shavings. Fixatives and oils remain as indicated. Prepare on the basis of the recipe for potpourri shown on page 29.

Flat, elongated fragrant parcels – also known as sachets – in wardrobes and bathroom closets not only have a very pleasant smell, but are also very useful in keeping undesirable pests away. All ingredients are powdered first of all in a mortar. For cushions, you should sew in an inner pocket (in cotton material) for the filling.

Sewing instructions for the parcel: Cut out a piece of material approximately 8 in by 8 in square. Stitch one edge (with a close zig-zag stitch, or alternatively fold the edge twice, ¹/₄ in each time, to the left and sew a narrow hem, or – if possible – use a sewing machine to sew on a decorative strip). Fold the material to the right, making half the width (the sewn edge should be on top), and then sew along the open long side and the unstitched short side. If necessary, sew along these edges with a zig-zag stitch. Turn inside out, half fill with a potpourri mixture and tie with a suitable band.

Sewing instructions for the scented heart: Cut out a rectangular piece of cloth with approximate dimensions of 8 x 4¹/₄ in. Fold the material on the shorter side to the right, making half the width. Then sew the remaining three sides, but leave a small hole for filling. Turn the material inside out. Fill the cushion loosely with potpourri. Sew up the filling hole. Holding one corner of the cushion firmly, gather the material together with your fingers and just above the diagonal line, tie it into a heart shape with a decorative band or cord.

Tip: With a combination of ²/₃ lavender and ¹/₃ oatmeal you can also make bath sachets (preferably out of tulle), ¹/₂ oz should be enough for two baths. Place the sachet directly in the water, or alternatively hang it on the faucet.

SACHETS

"Moth repellent" filling (intense, a little sharp):
1¹/₂ oz of each of the following: crushed artemisia, tansy and wormwood, together with ground santolina and feverfew.
1¹/₂ oz powdered orris root
10 drops of both lavender and myrtle oil
5 drops of both thyme and clove oil

PILLOWS

Filling I: (sleep promoting and relaxing effect)
2¹/₂ oz each of hops, lavender and balm
1¹/₂ oz powdered orris root
15 drops of both lavender and balm oil.

Filling II: (bewitching, alluring)
3 oz rose leaves
¹/₂ oz patchouli
¹/₂ oz each of powdered orris root, powdered cinnamon and coriander; mixed with:
a) 15 drops of jasmine oil,
5 drops of both geranium oil and Ylang-Ylang oil,
2 drops of musk oil

OR: (gently soothing)
b) 1¹/₂ oz of each of the following: hops, balm and lavender (with the same quantity of oatmeal or woolen fleece)
1¹/₂ oz powdered orris root,
3 drops of lavender oil,
1 drop of honey oil,
1 drop rose oil

INGREDIENTS – A SPIRAL OF SUNSHINE

4 oz ox-eye daisy petals and centers
20 drops of tonka oil
5 drops of both myrtle and mimosa oil.

INGREDIENTS – HARMONY IN WHITE

4 oz white flowers (such as elderflower, ranunculus, roses, hydrangea petals and florets)
$\frac{1}{2}$ oz rose leaves and quassia
5 vanilla pods (2 of which to be crushed)
$\frac{1}{2}$ oz allspice
$1\frac{1}{2}$ oz powdered orris root
10 drops of magnolia oil
5 drops each of the following oils: verbena, geranium and vanilla.

INGREDIENTS – FLAVORS OF THE ORIENT

4 oz flowers (such as peonies and roses)
$1\frac{1}{2}$ oz gum benjamin
15 drops of Ylang-Ylang oil
5 drops each of the following oils: cinnamon, bergamot and geranium
2 drops of musk oil.

INGREDIENTS – EXOTIC AND FARAWAY PLACES

3 oz fragrant wood (such as sandalwood, rosewood, cedar, madder or quassia)
3 oz spices (such as cinnamon, mace, cardamom, chili)
$\frac{1}{2}$ oz both patchouli and lavender
10 drops of sandalwood oil
5 drops each of the following oils: jasmine, rosewood, cedarwood, bay and patchouli.

A SPIRAL OF SUNSHINE

Mix 4 oz of ox-eye daisy petals and centers with the oils. This will give you a mixture containing at least one fixative oil (see ingredients). Arrange the daisy centers decoratively in the shape of a spiral on the bed of white petals.

HARMONY IN WHITE

This mixture of flowers and spices is particularly suitable for living rooms or reception areas. Lilies of the valley, roses, elderflower, strawflowers, ranunculus, hydrangea petals and other white flowers are placed in an arrangement of green rose leaves. The spice is provided by vanilla pods (see Ingredients), two of which should be added in crushed form, and allspice (see also the basic recipe for potpourri on page 29).

FLAVORS OF THE ORIENT

In addition to the mixture of flowers and spices shown under the Ingredients, the use of alder cones, hops, sage and mint, together with a bundle of cinnamon sticks, enhances the visual attraction of this potpourri. (See also the basic recipe for potpourri on page 29).

EXOTIC AND FARAWAY PLACES (BOUQUET)

Ingredients for the Bouquet: Peonies, wisteria, fresh bamboo branches, sweet peas, bamboo poles.
Preparation: Cut the flower stems and the branches, place in water.
Method: Cut the bamboo pole into lengths so that each piece is closed at one end in the form of a tube. (If this is not possible, block one end with a lump of putty.) Arrange these pieces so that they are parallel, but in any sequence, thickness or height, and tie them with raffia or a similar decorative strip, fill with water and arrange the flowers to your taste in the water.
Potpourri: Work the ingredients shown alongside as in the basic recipe for potpourri shown on page 29.

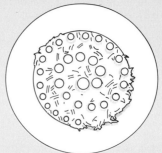

(A Spiral of Sunshine – see illustration on page 66)

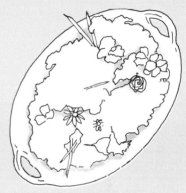

(Harmony in White – see illustration on page 67)

(Flavors of the Orient – see illustration on page 68)

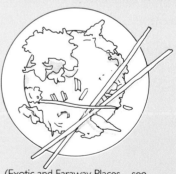

(Exotic and Faraway Places – see illustration on page 69)

A GIANT SPICE BOUQUET

Although this giant measures 36 inches across, the effect that it produces is by no means exaggerated. The combination of gentle colors and clearly arranged materials ensures that this arrangement remains subtle.

However, with a bouquet of this size, you must plan carefully where you are going to put it in your house. It smells beautiful! On the one hand, it evokes Christmas as do all spicy bouquets, but on the other, your choice of ingredients will determine the effect. For example, you could use ingredients that are likely to promote relaxation (for the living room), interest (for reception areas or entrances) or refreshment (for a dining room) and there are many different spices you could add.

Certainly a bouquet of this size will take a long time to prepare – roughly between 12 and 20 hours – but it will bring you a lot of joy for a long time to come.

You can, of course, adapt this design to any size to suit your requirements.

Fragrance note: Full of Christmas spices, together with whatever else you choose to create a fragrant and eye-catching decoration for your Christmas festivities.

CLASSICAL SPICE BOUQUETS

In this example, the characteristic "gingerbread scent" of spice bouquets is matched with a fine blend of colors and luxurious materials. The overall effect of the spice posy is reinforced by the antique letter stand and the wooden bowl.

Together with the wall-mounted bouquet, this quiet and dignified composition demonstrates the painstaking and time-consuming nature of this highly individual handiwork.

Fragrance note: Christmas spices with a hint of clove and cinnamon

Because of the visual effect of its weight, the wall-mounted bouquet on the right was arranged with the stem pointing upwards.

A MODERN SPICE BOUQUET

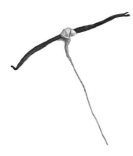

The combination of dainty tendrils from the sweet pea plant with strong cinnamon sticks is a perfect complement in this fresh bouquet. It is supported in the center by orange blossom, freesias, roses and sweet peas, creating a harmonious balance of fresh, flowery and spicy perfumes. The interesting lines of the tendrils are visually offset by the golden wire mesh with its added spices. It is really very simple to construct a bouquet like this using a "framework" of wired cinnamon sticks and ginger roots.

Fragrance note: Sweetly fresh blossom scents with a spicy tang of cinnamon

Fragrance note: Spicy,
attractively sweet and piquant.

Now that you have seen a fresh bouquet, here is another that has been dried. I left it in a vase of water, about 2 inches deep, to ensure that the flowers dried out very slowly. I filled the gaps produced in the bouquet during the drying process with additional tendrils, lily of the valley leaves and roses. The fragile effect of the spices is enhanced by that of the dried flowers and is in direct contrast with the silky sheen of the Indian drape.

In the lower illustrations you can see the preparation of the flat, tied bouquet from the initial wiring stage right through to the final assembly of the framework. These basic techniques are described in the chapters that deal with "Wiring" (pages 22/23) and "Tying Bouquets and Sprays" (pages 24/25) and also in the method for creating this bouquet on page 79.

The basic framework of the bouquet is made from long cinnamon sticks, fresh ginger roots and a vanilla pod. The intervening spaces are filled with fresh flowers. Gossamer-like, the decorative wire mesh, studded with tiny fragments of spice, surrounds the final bouquet.

(A Giant Spice Bouquet – see illustration on pages 72/73)

(Classical Spice Bouquets – see illustration on pages 74/75)

A GIANT SPICE BOUQUET

Ingredients: Miscellaneous spices (such as cinnamon, nutmeg, star anise), dried flowers (here, I have used teasel heads, cockscombs, rose-hips among others), floristry adhesive tape and dry foam.

Preparation: Wire the spices and dried flowers as shown on pages 22/23 (except for the roses and the teasel heads). Make sure that the wired components of each type are much the same size, so that your rings are regular.

Method: Ideally, this bouquet needs to be stuck. To do this, you will need a flat dish, across both sides of which you should arrange the adhesive tape. Stick onto this the dry-foam, which you should cut flat and to a thickness of about 6in in the center and 2in on the outside. The container must be completely filled. If you want, you can break up the dry-foam into smaller pieces. Starting in the center and working outward insert the wired spices and dried flowers making a ring. But please note, you will have to interrupt the ring-shaped pattern from time to time as otherwise the effect will be too monotonous. This final stage of the bouquet is formed from interwoven pliable stems, say from honeysuckle and the red stems of the dogwood which are wired together at a number of points. This bouquet stands on a pedestal which has been covered with dry branches.

CLASSICAL SPICE BOUQUETS

Ingredients: Miscellaneous spices, seed heads, pine cones, dried flowers and foliage, a bar of wood, floristry tape, decorative wire, mounting wire, a roll of winding wire, cotton wool.

Method for the spice posy: Choose an attractive flower for the centerpiece of your bouquet. Arrange the wired foliage and the spices around this in the shape of a ring. Tightly bind the bundle with winding wire. Leave the wire on the roll, making sure that a short length protrudes. Working slightly downward, continue to arrange the bound spices in circles, securing each row with

WIRING RIBBONS

Fashion a wire hook from a length of supporting wire. Then taking a length of ribbon in one hand, allow one end to hang down and to form a loop. With your other hand, make a second loop on the right hand side and then bring it together with the first loop. Then wind the wire around the lower part of the loops and place the wire hook around the gathered center. You will now have to wind the longer end of the ribbon around the shorter end just below the loop. Loops like this can be put to many uses.

With classical spice bouquets, the spices, seed heads, dried flowers and foliage. should be wired as shown on pages 22/23 before the bouquets are tied. You should also prepare all decorative wire and artificial flowers beforehand.

DECORATIVE WIRE FLOWERS

To make a decorative wire flower, take 5 pieces of decorative golden wire (approximately 2–3 in in length) and fashion them into oval leaf shapes, twisting the ends together to form a $1/2$ in long "stem". Wind the mounting wire around each leaf, twisting the ends several times around the stem left by the decorative wire. Assemble the leaves and stick either a small pearl or a clove in the center.

COLLARS

If you want to include a collar for your bouquet, you can slide this firmly up over the stems of the finished bouquet. Finally, place a small pad of cotton wool over the ends of the wire (to prevent any damage) and bind the stem with floristry tape so that at the top the collar cannot slip and at the bottom the cotton wool pad is concealed.

TIP FOR A MODERN SPICE BOUQUET

Those stems that have been wired and bound with tape should be cut a little shorter than the flower stems. Once the bouquet has dried, just add flowers and re-tie the bouquet.

the winding wire (you will need roughly twice the quantity of wire for each successive circle). The horizontal connections are now assured by means of small wired bunches of foliage. Then cut the winding wire and twist both ends securely together. Using a pair of wire clippers, you should cut the wire ends from time to time to match the length of the stem in the final bouquet.

METHOD FOR THE WALL-MOUNTED SPICE BOUQUET

Gather together and wire the bunches consisting of wired spices, seed heads, cones, artificial flowers, spice and/or decorative wire flowers and wind them around the wooden bar, on the right, the left and the center (making the lower bunches progressively larger). Cover the end of the stems with floristry tape and decorate with a large bow.

A MODERN SPICE BOUQUET

Ingredients: Large cinnamon sticks, fresh ginger root, vanilla pods, leaves, small spices, decorative wire, fragrant flowers (here, I have used freesia, sweet peas, roses and orange blossom).
Preparation: The spices should be wired as shown on pages 22/23. Wrap the smaller items in the decorative wire until you have a large tendril.
Method: Start with the long cinnamon sticks and place these across each other in such a way that you can gather the ends of wire together. Then add the (fresh) ginger roots on one side and insert the wire with the vanilla pod downward from the top. There will be a number of gaps in the middle and you should fill these with fresh flowers. These fresh flowers will make up the centerpiece of the arrangement. The curved flowers to be used for the horizontal lines should be placed between and below the cinnamon sticks and the ginger roots. These latter will support the flowers and prevent them from becoming displaced. Then wind the wire mesh of spice around the finished bouquet. When tying the bouquet, make sure you include the lower ends of the wire mesh.

(Classical Spice Bouquets – see illustration on pages 74/75)

(A Modern Spice Bouquet – see illustration on pages 76/77)